Science Alive

Electricity

Terry Jennings

Smart Apple Media

Smart Apple Media is published by Black Rabbit Books
P.O. Box 3263, Mankato, Minnesota 56002

Printed in China
Created by Q2A Media
Series Editor: Honor Head
Book Editor: Harriet McGregor
Senior Art Designers: Ashita Murgai, Nishant Mudgal
Designer: Harleen Mehta
Picture Researcher: Poloumi Ghosh
Line Artists: Indernil Ganguly, Rishi Bhardhwaj
Illustrators: Kusum Kala, Sanyogita Lal

Library of Congress Cataloging-in-Publication Data

Jennings, Terry J.
    Electricity / Terry Jennings.
    p. cm.—(Smart Apple Media. Science alive)
    Summary: "Explains essential facts about electricity, including static electricity, electric currents, circuits, and batteries. Includes experiments"—Provided by publisher.
    Includes index.
    ISBN 978-1-59920-271-6
    1. Electricity—Experiments—Juvenile literature. I. Title.
QC527.2.J454 2009
537—dc22
                                                                                        2007049120

All words in **bold** can be found in "Words to Remember" on pages 30–31.

Web site information is correct at time of going to press. However, the publishers cannot accept liability for any information or links found on third-party web sites.
Picture credits
t=top b=bottom c=center l=left r=right m=middle
Cover Images: Main Image: Bubbles Photolibrary / Alamy   Small Image: Wouter Tolenaars / Shutterstock:
Atlantide Phototravel/ Corbis: 4, MvH/ istockphoto: 7, Milos Luzanin/ Shutterstock: 11,
H. Schmid/ zefa/ Corbis: 15, Juniors Bildarchiv/ Photolibrary: 18, Richard T Nowitz/ Photolibrary: 19,
paulaphoto/ Shutterstock: 20, Edward Hardam/ Shutterstock: 21, flashon/ Shutterstock: 25,
Vlad Valeyev/ Shutterstock: 26, Scholastic Studio 10/ Photolibrary: 28, Tihis/ Shutterstock: 29

9 8 7 6 5 4 3 2 1

Contents

What Is Electricity?

Electricity is a type of **energy.** Electricity gives power, light, and heat to cities, towns, and villages all over the world.

Sparks and Currents

There are two types of electricity. You can see one type of electricity when you comb your hair and it stands on end. This is called **static electricity.** The other type of electricity flows through wires. This is called **current electricity.**

▲ *Current electricity makes these colorful signs light up.*

Changing Energy

Electricity can be changed into other types of energy. In a light bulb, electricity is changed into light. In an electric heater, electricity is changed into heat.

◀ *Electricity travels from a plug through a wire and powers this lamp. Electrical energy has changed into light and heat energy.*

Static Electricity

The first type of electricity that scientists discovered was **static electricity**. Static means to stay still. Static electricity usually stays in one place.

Rubbing

Static electricity is made when two materials rub together. Have you heard crackling sounds when you undress? That is static electricity. It is made when your clothes rub against you.

▼ *Static electricity attracts your hair to a comb. It usually happens when the weather is dry. If the weather is damp, you may not see the effects of static electricity.*

Electricity in the Clouds

Lightning is also caused by static electricity. It builds up in storm clouds. When there is too much static electricity, it leaps to another cloud or to the ground. You see it as a flash of lightning.

▲ *Lightning is caused by static electricity. It is extremely powerful.*

Try This...

Jumping Paper

You can find out more about static electricity by doing this simple experiment.

You will need

• tissue paper • scissors • a fuzzy sweater • a balloon

1 Cut or tear the tissue paper into tiny pieces, the smaller the better.

2 Blow up the balloon. Rub it on the sweater.

3 Hold the balloon just above the pieces of paper.

What happened?

When you rubbed the balloon, static electricity collected on the balloon's surface. This means that the balloon became charged with static electricity. The paper was attracted to the charged balloon.

Currents

Electricity is most useful when it flows along a wire. This is called an **electric current.** An electric current can power machines.

Circuits

A circuit is a path or loop that electricity can flow around. If you make a loop by connecting wires to a light bulb and to a **battery,** the bulb lights up. You have made an electric circuit. Electricity flows from the battery, through the bulb, and back to the battery.

Battery

Wire

Bulb

▲ *The battery produces an electric current. The battery pushes the electric current around the circuit.*

Conductors and Insulators

Materials that allow an electric current to flow through them are called **conductors.** Metals, such as copper and gold, are good conductors. **Insulators** are materials that an electric current cannot flow through easily. Plastic and rubber are good insulators.

▶ *An electric cable is made from a conductor and an insulator. The electric current flows through the metal conductor. The plastic insulator stops the electric current from escaping.*

Plastic insulator

Copper conductor

Try This...
Electric Circuits

You can see how an electrical circuit works by building one.

You Will Need

• a wooden or plastic tray • a battery • two metal paper clips • tape • two wires • a flashlight bulb • a selection of objects—keys, coins, string, rubber bands, paper, paper clips

1 Set up the equipment on the tray as shown in the drawing.

Paper clip

Battery

Tape

Wire

Free end of wire

Bulb

2 Touch the free end of the wire to the metal end of the bulb.

Bulb

Battery

Wire

Rubber band connecting the wire and bulb

3 Touch the free end of the wire against one end of one of your objects. Touch the other end of the object against the metal end of the bulb.

Repeat this with your other objects.

What happened?

When the wire touches the bulb, the circuit is complete. The battery pushes an electric current around the circuit. The bulb lights. When you connect some objects in the circuit, the bulb does not light. These objects are insulators. When you connect other objects in the circuit, the bulb lights. These objects are conductors.

Using Switches

We use electrical machines to do work for us at home. They heat water, wash clothes, clean dishes, and suck dust off the floor. We turn them on and off with a **switch.**

On and Off

When a switch is on, it completes the circuit and an electric current flows. When a switch is off, it makes a gap in the circuit. The electric current stops flowing.

Battery

Wire

No current flowing

Switch "off"

Switch "on"

Current flowing

Powerful Electricity

The electricity that is wired into our homes is very powerful. Be careful when unplugging and plugging in machines. Never play around with electricity.

◀ *Electricity is powerful enough to work large machines, such as this washing machine.*

Try This...
Series and Parallel

See what happens when you add extra bulbs to a circuit.

You Will Need
• a battery • six pieces of wire • tape
• metal paper clips • three flashlight bulbs in bulb holders • a small screwdriver

1 Make a circuit like the one in the picture. This is called a series circuit because the bulbs are in a series, or row.

2 Now add an extra bulb to the circuit. Are the bulbs brighter or dimmer than before? Ask an adult to remove one of the bulbs. What happens to the other bulbs?

3 Now wire three bulbs like this. This is called a parallel circuit. Are the bulbs brighter or dimmer than before? Ask an adult to remove one of the bulbs. What happens to the other bulbs?

What happened?

In the series circuit, an extra bulb makes all the bulbs dimmer since they share the electrical current. When you remove one bulb, the other bulbs go out. In the parallel circuit, all the bulbs are equally bright. If one bulb is removed, the others stay lit. Which type of circuit do you think you have in your home?

Electric Animals

A few animals use electricity when they hunt for food. Some animals even use electricity to attack other creatures.

Electric Fish

Electric currents flow through water. Some fish can sense electricity coming from their prey (animals they eat). They can even find animals hidden under sand.

▼ *The hammerhead shark uses its strangely shaped head to sense electric signals underwater.*

Zap!

The electric eel has muscles that can produce electricity. The eel can stun its prey with a powerful electric shock. If another animal attacks an electric eel... ZAP!

▲ *Some electric eels grow to more than 3 feet (1 m) in length. Electric eels can store electricity like a battery.*

Batteries and Bulbs

Batteries are containers filled with chemicals. They make electricity. All sorts of gadgets, such as watches, cell phones, and cameras are powered by batteries.

▶ *Batteries let you use a laptop computer without having to plug it in.*

Chemicals

A battery turns chemicals into electrical energy. When you turn on a flashlight, electricity flows along a strip of metal from the battery to the bulb. The bulb glows. The battery makes electricity until its chemicals have been used up.

Bulbs

Electricity heats up the materials that it flows through. Inside some light bulbs is a very thin wire called a filament. When electricity flows through the filament, it becomes so hot that it glows brightly.

Filament

▶ *You can see the thin filament in the center of the light bulb. It eventually burns out and the light bulb must be replaced.*

Try This...
Making Batteries

You can find out more about batteries by making one from a few simple materials.

You Will Need
• a lemon • a clean paper clip • a clean penny

 Squeeze and roll a lemon to make it juicier. Ask an adult to make two small slits in the lemon's skin.

2 Thoroughly wash the paper clip and the penny. Push the paper clip into one slit and push the penny into the other slit. They should not touch each other.

3 Put your tongue on the paper clip and the penny. Your tongue must touch both objects at the same time.

What happened?

When the metals touch the lemon juice, a chemical reaction begins. The reaction pushes an electric current from the paper clip to the penny. When you touch them with your tongue, you make a complete circuit. You may feel a tingle as the tiny current crosses your tongue. **Never try this with any other electricity source.**

Power Plants

Most of the electricity we use in our homes, stores, factories, and streets is made in large buildings called **power plants.**

Steam Power

Most power plants burn fuel, such as coal, oil, or gas, to heat water. The water changes to steam. It rushes through pipes and hits paddle-wheels called **turbines.** The steam makes the turbines spin. The turbines drive huge electricity **generators,** which produce electricity.

Coal

Steam travels to turbine

Generator makes electricity

Furnace

Water

Turbine

Cables

Electricity leaves the power plant and travels along cables to wherever it is needed. Tall towers called pylons hold the cables above the ground. In cities, the cables may be below the ground.

◀ It is important to stay away from pylons. They carry huge amounts of electricity and can be very dangerous.

Green Electricity

Burning fuels to make electricity produces gases that collect in the air. They are making Earth warmer. This is called **global warming.** Some ways of making electricity do not cause global warming. They are called "green" because they are earth-friendly.

Water Power

The energy of moving water can be used to make electricity. A **dam** is built across a river so that a **reservoir** forms. Water from the reservoir passes through turbines. The turbines turn and spin generators. The generators produce electricity.

▲ *This dam makes electricity for homes, factories, stores, and schools.*

Wind Energy

A **wind turbine** looks like a giant fan on top of a tall tower. The wind energy turns the blades and this drives a generator. The generator produces electricity.

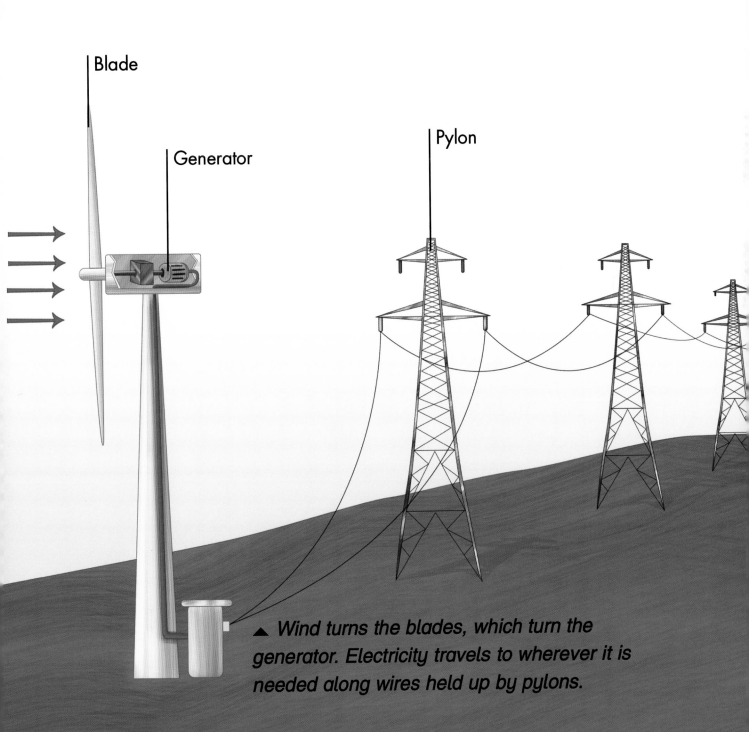

Blade

Generator

Pylon

▲ *Wind turns the blades, which turn the generator. Electricity travels to wherever it is needed along wires held up by pylons.*

Electronics

Sound, pictures, and messages can all be changed into electricity. They can be sent a long way very quickly.

Telephones

When you speak into a telephone, the sound is changed into electrical signals. These go down the wire to another telephone. The second telephone turns the electrical signals back into sounds.

◀ *Cell phones are electronic and need electricity to work. They send their signals through the air as radio waves.*

Computers

A computer works using **microchips.** Microchips are tiny electrical circuits. They act as the computer's brain and its memory.

▲ *Each tiny rectangle here is a microchip. Each microchip contains thousands of electronic parts.*

Words to Remember

Battery

A device that uses chemical energy to make electricity.

Conductor

A material that allows electricity to pass through it easily.

Dam

A wall built across a river valley to hold back water.

Electric current

An electrical charge that moves through a wire.

Energy

The ability to do work, such as giving heat, light, and moving things.

Generator

A machine that changes movement energy into electricity.

Global warming

The warming of Earth's atmosphere. Most scientists believe global warming is caused by gases produced when people burn coal, oil, and gas.

Insulator

A material that does not allow electricity to pass through it.

Microchip

An electronic circuit containing lots of tiny parts.

Power plant

A building where electricity is made and sent out for people to use.

Reservoir

A man-made lake often created by a dam.

Static electricity

Electricity that builds up on the surface of materials that do not conduct electricity.

Switch

A device that turns an electric current on and off.

Turbine

A set of blades that spins when water, steam, or air pushes against it. Turbines are often connected to generators.

Wind turbine

A machine that uses wind energy to produce electricity.

Index

Web Finder

For Kids:

http://scifiles.larc.nasa.gov/text/kids/D_Lab/acts_electric.html

http://www.aecl.ca/kidszone/atomicenergy/electricity/index.asp

http://www.eso.qld.gov.au/electricity/html/activities.html

For Teachers:

http://www.teach-nology.com/teachers/lesson_plans/science/physics/electricity/

http://www1.eere.energy.gov/education/lesson_plans.html

http://www.energy.gov/foreducators.htm